THIS BOOK

BELONGS

TO

_____

HEY, POOPIE!

LIFE, PUBERTY, *Then* THE PURSUIT *of* HAPPINESS

BY REAL-LIFE CHRIS

Trafford
PUBLISHING

www.trafford.com

North America & international
toll-free: 1 888 232 4444 (USA & Canada)
phone: 250 383 6864 ◆ fax: 812 355 4082

FOR MOM & JERRY

HEY, POOPIE!

LIFE, PUBERTY, *Then* THE PURSUIT *of* HAPPINESS

BY REAL LIFE CHRIS

Trafford
PUBLISHING™

2

6

7

13

16

35

36

37

40

46

50

65

68

85

86

119

123

129

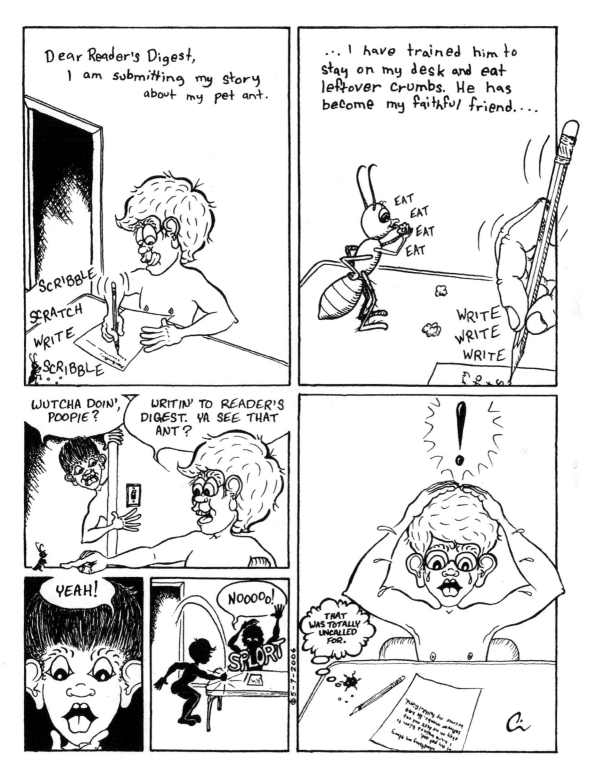

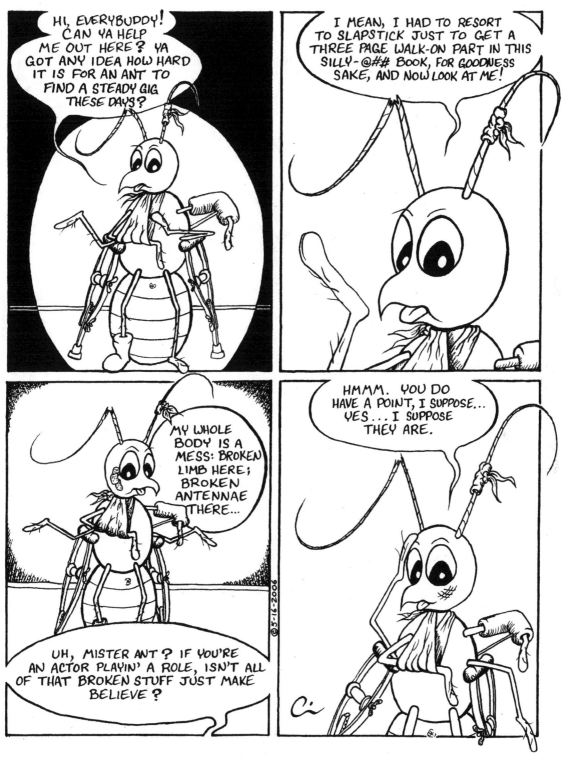

136

153

157

159

162

164

❧About the Author☙

The author of this book has such a fragile ego and insatiable need for acceptance that he is actually writing his own "About the Author" notes. By "he," of course, I mean "me." So read this shamelessly self-serving diatribe about ME, ME, ME, and then like me. You may even want to send me money. But enough about that; now more about *meeee!*

Although the author has always been a devoted fan of such gifted cartoonists as Charles Schulz (Peanuts), Johnny Hart (B.C.), Berkeley Breathed (Bloom County, Outland, Opus), Darby Conley (Get Fuzzy), and Stephan Pastis (Pearls Before Swine), he never considered a career as a cartoonist until the age of 41. For most of his life Chris Shirley, A.K.A. "Real Life Chris," had enjoyed a successful career as a photographer by day, and a night-club singer by night. He was only 5 years old when he decided to dedicate his life to making music, but truth be told, his underlying motive for this decision was to get close to an older man in his neighborhood who played guitar, and with whom Chris had fallen deeply in love. The older man was 6.

In Chris's defense, it is a widely accepted notion that 92% of all guitarists become guitarists for the sole purpose of getting laid.* Okay, so maybe getting laid wasn't exactly what 5-year-old Chris had in mind, but his decision *was* made for the love of another man, and that was just the beginning of *sooooo* many things to come, including **_HEY, POOPIE!_**

---

* margin of error ± 8% (source of statistic: I made it up)

Coming Soon